HOW TO DRAW

DRAGONBALL Z

Greatest Heroes & Villains

by Maria B. Alfano
Illustrated by Ron Zalme

* *

SCHOLASTIC INC.

New York   Toronto   London   Auckland   Sydney   Mexico City   ~~Hong Kong~~   ~~Buenos~~ Aires

ISBN-13: 978-0-545-00135-9
ISBN-10: 0-545-00135-8

Published by Scholastic Inc.
SCHOLASTIC and associated logos are trademarks and/or registered trademarks of Scholastic Inc.

Designed by Phil Falco

12 11 10 9 8 7 6 5 4 3   8 9 10/0

Printed in the U.S.A.
First printing, November 2007

Join the battle.
Defend the Earth.

Learn to draw your favorite DBZ heroes and villains!

✱✱✱

What are the top three secrets of Super Saiyan drawing masters?

- Start each drawing in pencil. Keep your lines light and loose until you are almost finished. This will make it easy to draw over them.

- Even drawings of the most complicated characters start with the same two guidelines: One long vertical line that runs right down the center of the body — like a spine or backbone — and one horizontal line where the shoulders will be.

- Relax and have fun! If you're too afraid of messing up, you'll never know how great you can be!

✱✱✱

BREAK IT DOWN

Think hands and faces are the hardest parts of a drawing? Try sketching hands and faces on scrap paper before you move on. Practice like you're training for the International Martial Arts Tournament. It's the only way to gain Super Saiyan drawing skills!

✱ ✱

Hands

○ Draw a circle or oval.

○ Lightly draw the general shapes.

○ Sketch in the fingers

○ Add details, like creases where the fingers bend, to make hands look realistic.

Faces

○ Start with an oval. Then divide the oval with two guidelines. These guidelines help you figure out which way a character is facing. They also let you know where to draw the eyes, nose, and mouth.

Keep in mind that the vertical guideline runs down the middle of the FACE, not the middle of the oval. It falls between the eyes and through the center of the nose and mouth. It cuts the oval in half only if the character is facing forward.

A horizontal guideline shows where the eyes will be. It's not usually in the middle of the oval, either. Flip through the book and take a look!

○ Use the guidelines to place the eyes, mouth, and ears. Start with simple shapes.

○ Now start adding details.

○ Quick short lines between the eyes, on the cheeks, and under the chin make the face more realistic.

Training complete! You're ready for your first DBZ drawing challenge.

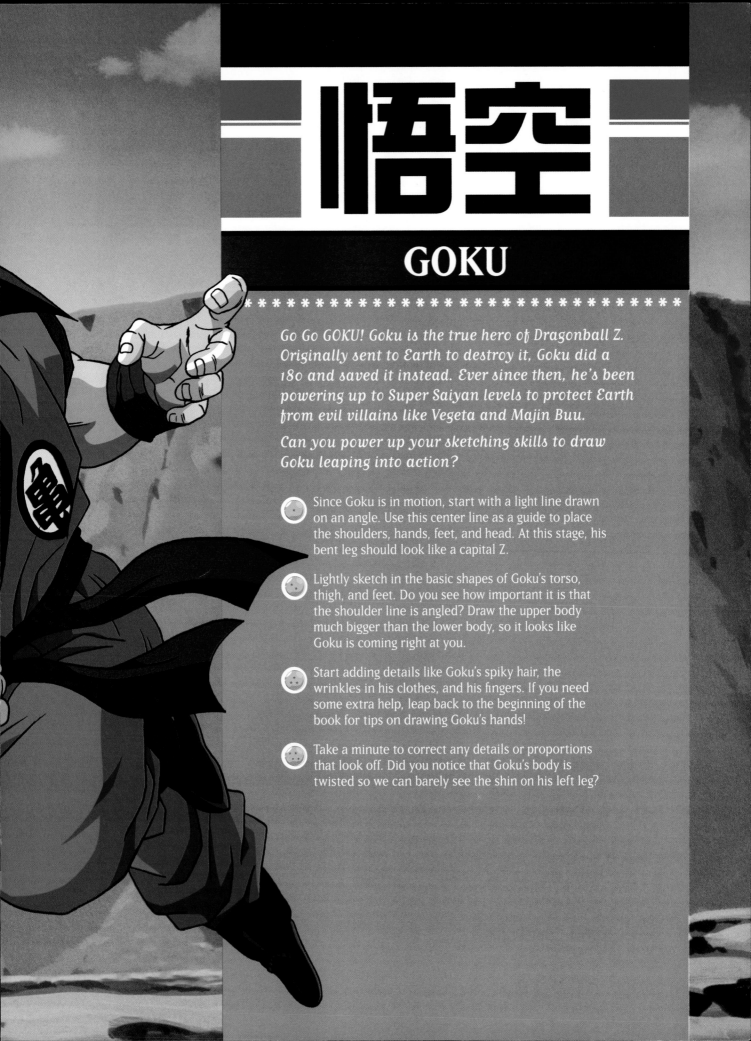

悟空

GOKU

✴ ✴

Go Go GOKU! Goku is the true hero of Dragonball Z. Originally sent to Earth to destroy it, Goku did a 180 and saved it instead. Ever since then, he's been powering up to Super Saiyan levels to protect Earth from evil villains like Vegeta and Majin Buu.

Can you power up your sketching skills to draw Goku leaping into action?

Since Goku is in motion, start with a light line drawn on an angle. Use this center line as a guide to place the shoulders, hands, feet, and head. At this stage, his bent leg should look like a capital Z.

Lightly sketch in the basic shapes of Goku's torso, thigh, and feet. Do you see how important it is that the shoulder line is angled? Draw the upper body much bigger than the lower body, so it looks like Goku is coming right at you.

Start adding details like Goku's spiky hair, the wrinkles in his clothes, and his fingers. If you need some extra help, leap back to the beginning of the book for tips on drawing Goku's hands!

Take a minute to correct any details or proportions that look off. Did you notice that Goku's body is twisted so we can barely see the shin on his left leg?

ピッコロ

PICCOLO

* *

Power up Piccolo! Piccolo is best known for his powerful energy blasts and his ability to split into two or four separate beings. But he also has the super-cool ability to regenerate any limbs he loses in battle.

You can power up for this drawing challenge by stretching out your arms and sharpening your pencil.

- The trick to making Piccolo's left hand look like it's coming right at you is to draw it much bigger than you think it should be. Deal with the size right away by sketching the oval for the right hand almost as big as the oval for the head. And look closely: The left leg gets a bigger curve than the right leg because it pushes forward.

- Sketch in the basic shapes of the body and cape. Remember to use light, loose lines so you can erase them later. The head tips forward, so the top of the head and the top of the shoulders are on the same line.

- Give your pencil a workout with all those details — like the turban on Piccolo's head and the lines on his arms. Then clean up the outlines.

- Erase any lines you don't need. Now step back and evaluate your drawing. If you sit too close, it will be harder to spot mistakes. Did you draw short lines on the fingers to show where they bend? Did you draw a V between the eyes to show concentration?

スーパーサイヤ人 悟空

SUPER SAIYAN GOKU

✳✳✳✳✳✳✳✳✳✳✳✳✳✳✳✳✳✳✳✳✳✳✳✳✳✳✳✳✳✳✳

Battling fierce enemies to save the Earth is no easy task. Goku has to power up to fighting levels so high, it turns his hair blond and his eyes green! Becoming a Super Saiyan used up so much of Goku's energy, he didn't have enough left over to learn the art of fusion. Do you have enough energy to take on this drawing?

⊙ Set up your drawing. Start with a sweeping center line and tilted, curved shoulder and hip lines. Use these guidelines to place the head. Take your time and make sure you've got your drawing set up before you move on. Is the right leg long and outstretched? Is the back leg bent? Where are the hands and feet?

⊙ Sketch the basic shapes. See how the shoulders come out from behind the head? Take a minute to look at how the shapes connect to one another. Then start drawing in Goku's hair and face.

⊙ Now that you've got the basics down, refine the outlines and start adding small details. V-shaped lines show drapes in the pants, short curved lines show muscles on the arms. If you're having trouble at this stage, it might be time to take a tracing break. Tracing isn't cheating – it's a great way to practice a complicated drawing.

⊙ Reality check. Are you happy with the outlines? Did you get all the details down? Is the right leg bigger than the left leg, as it should be? Excellent! What about the powerful look in Goku's eyes? Now erase any lines you don't need.

* *

Stop the clock! Trunks is from the future — a horrible future where evil androids rule the Earth. But he's zipped back to the present day to stop those androids in their tracks. Shouldn't be a problem for a warrior who can turn Super Saiyan at will!

Ever wanted to know how to show movement in your drawing? This is your chance, so get ready for action!

Super Saiyan Trunks's whole body is twisted, so start out with a curved center guideline. Tilt the hip line up at an angle. Then attach the arms and legs — they are bent for battle.

Sketch the body around the guidelines. Remember, the vertical line runs right down the center of the body. Don't forget to add in a swoop of hair moving to his right and to sketch the outline of his sword. Keep your lines light and your grip loose: Move your entire arm as you draw — not just your wrist.

This drawing is starting to get intense! If you want to smudge-proof your masterpiece, keep a piece of scrap paper under your hand as you clean up the outlines and focus on the details. Did you get all the wrinkles in the fabric, and bulges in the muscles?

Erase any lines you don't need and make final changes. Did you add all the detail lines on the sword? Does the hair look like the wind is blowing it back?

グレート サイヤマン

GREAT SAIYAMAN

* *

Who's hiding behind that helmet? Could it be Goku's teenage son, Gohan? During high school, Gohan adopts a secret identity when fighting bad guys. And all he has to do to transform himself is push a button on his super-cool Transformation Band Watch.

- Draw a proud stick figure with circles for hands and triangles for feet. Look at the guidelines for the face. Can you see how it already looks like the head is tipping forward? Getting the basics on target in this step will help you to draw a super-realistic Great Saiyaman!

- Lightly lay in the shapes — the angular shapes of the tunic, boots, and arms and the triangular cape. Take your time setting up the helmet. You might even want to practice on a bit of scrap paper first. This is new territory!

- Now that you've got the basics down, go back and adjust the outlines. Then start adding details like the curves in the knees and folds in the fabric. Folds show where clothing either hangs or stretches. So if a character is standing still, gravity will pull the fold downward — like the U-shaped folds in Great Saiyaman's green tunic.

- Time for the final check! Did you catch all those details, like the antennae on the helmet and the Transformation Band Watch? Are the arms and legs the right size and shape? Erase any lines you don't need and correct any that aren't quite right.

GOTEN

* *

Go for it, Goten! Goten is one of Goku's two sons. Like his father, he loves training in the martial arts and defending the Earth from evil. His biggest accomplishment is fusing with his best buddy, Trunks, to form the super-powerful Gotenks.

Start by drawing a vertical guideline. Then draw horizontal lines where the shoulders and hips should be. Use these to place the head, hands, and feet. Then draw more guidelines on the face. Think of this step as a pumped-up stick figure.

Lightly sketch an upside-down triangle for the torso on top of the guidelines. Then connect the simple shapes of the arms and legs to this triangle.

Start adding details, like Goten's spiky hair, the drapes in his clothing, and his fists of steel. Don't forget the eyebrows! Not sure where a line is supposed to be? Take a look at the finished drawing to help you understand what to do next — or just for inspiration.

Now, erase any lines you don't need. Next, finish up the details. Did you draw the lines under his eyes for cheeks and that knot in his belt?

GREAT JOB! You've just powered through your first DBZ drawing challenge. Keep up the good work!

スーパーサイヤ人3
ゴテンクス

SUPER SAIYAN 3 GOTENKS

When two warriors of equal size and strength merge into one kick-butt super-powerful force, that's fusion. Gotenks is the fused form of Goten and Trunks and combines all their awesome skills into one incredible fighting form. These warriors had to focus and train hard to fuse, but once they mastered it, their power went through the roof! Gotenks learns new moves so quickly, he went to Super Saiyan 3 after watching Goku do it just ONCE!

Don't worry, you might not perfect this drawing on the first try, but you've still got SUPER SAIYAN 3 skills!

Super Saiyan 3 Gotenks is hunched over, so start with a curved vertical line. Use it as a guide to sketch a stick-figure version of the final drawing. Did you notice the head is so low that it overlaps the shoulders? Later on, the nose and mouth will actually fall BELOW the shoulder line, so it's important to draw the oval in the right spot.

This drawing gets detailed right away. Take it slow. Lightly sketch in the basic body shapes and a big sweeping line for that mass of hair. Keep in mind that Gotenks is turning to the side, so there's more body to the right of the center line than there is to the left of it.

You've got the basics down. Move on to the details. Take some extra time to focus on the face.

Break time! Step back and take a look at your drawing. Erase lines you don't need and add finishing touches. Did you draw the detail lines in his hair, above his brow, and on his chest?

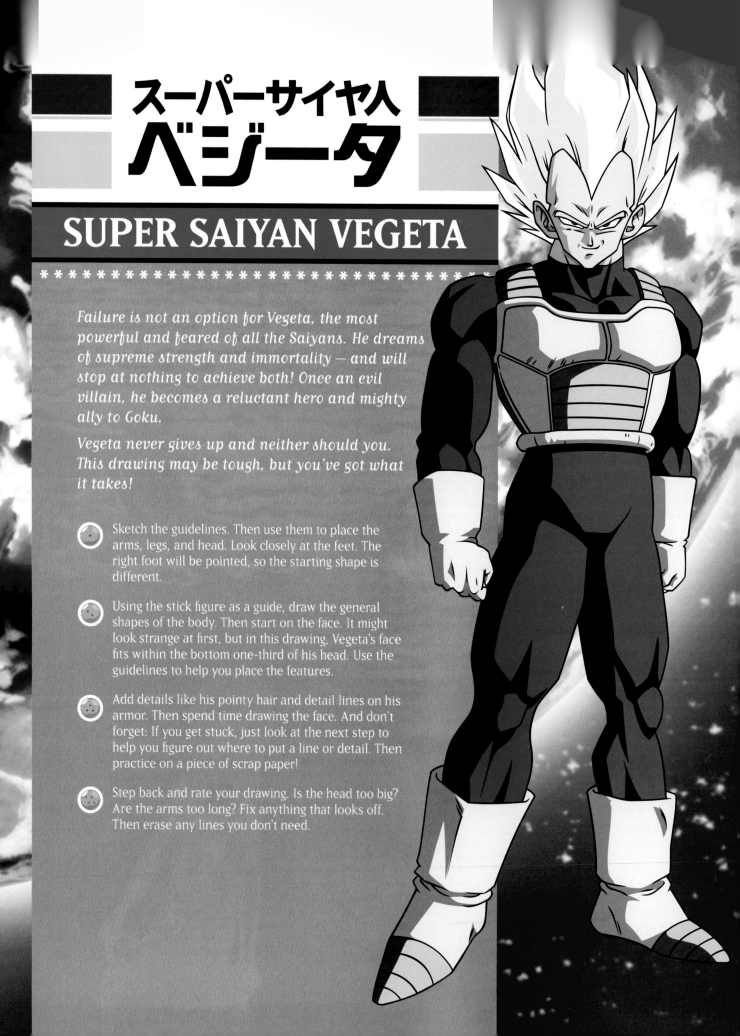

スーパーサイヤ人
ベジータ

SUPER SAIYAN VEGETA

* *

Failure is not an option for Vegeta, the most powerful and feared of all the Saiyans. He dreams of supreme strength and immortality — and will stop at nothing to achieve both! Once an evil villain, he becomes a reluctant hero and mighty ally to Goku.

Vegeta never gives up and neither should you. This drawing may be tough, but you've got what it takes!

- Sketch the guidelines. Then use them to place the arms, legs, and head. Look closely at the feet. The right foot will be pointed, so the starting shape is different.

- Using the stick figure as a guide, draw the general shapes of the body. Then start on the face. It might look strange at first, but in this drawing, Vegeta's face fits within the bottom one-third of his head. Use the guidelines to help you place the features.

- Add details like his pointy hair and detail lines on his armor. Then spend time drawing the face. And don't forget: If you get stuck, just look at the next step to help you figure out where to put a line or detail. Then practice on a piece of scrap paper!

- Step back and rate your drawing. Is the head too big? Are the arms too long? Fix anything that looks off. Then erase any lines you don't need.

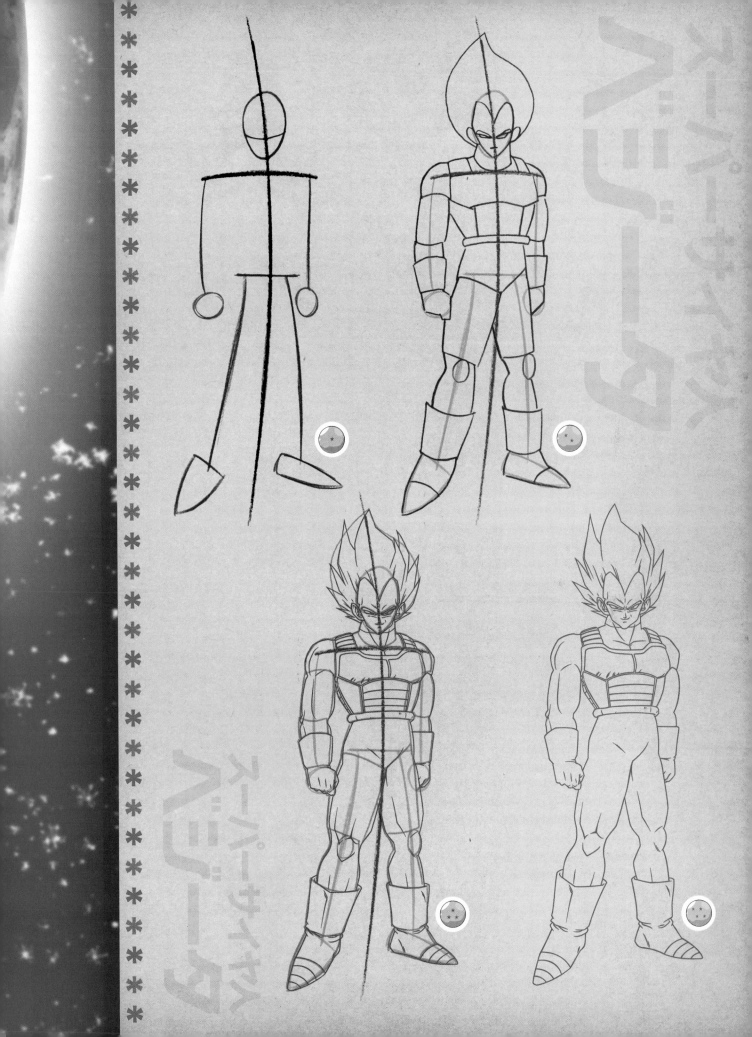

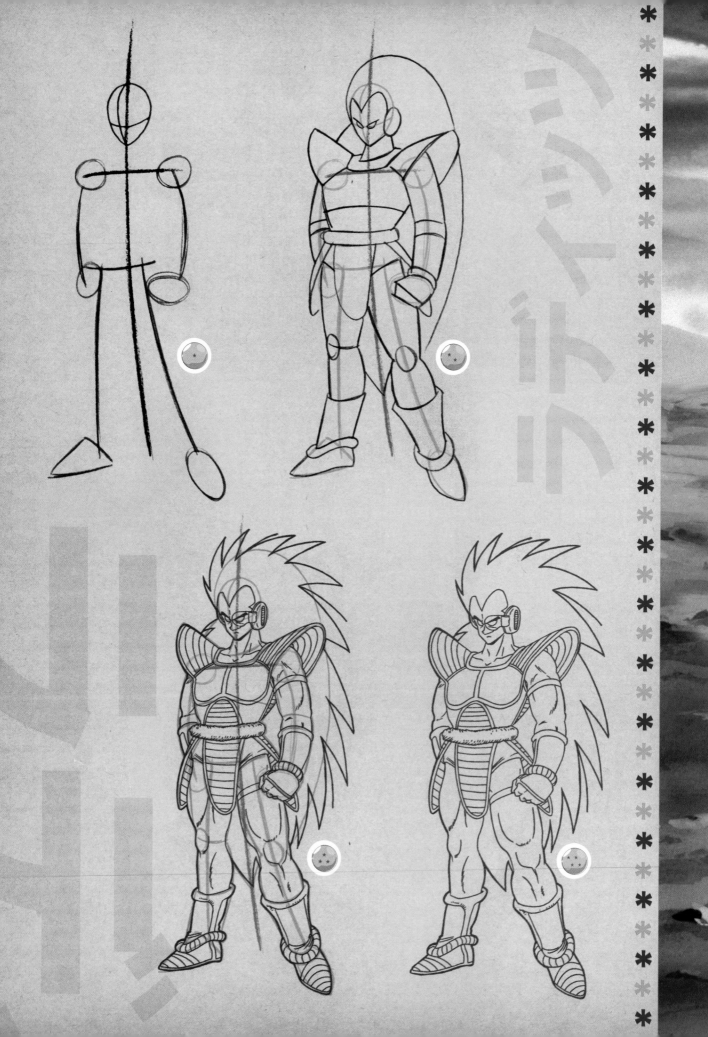

ラディッツ

RADITZ

* *

Angry, intolerant, and super-mean, Raditz is Goku's evil big brother and his complete opposite. Raditz came to Earth with one mission: to destroy it. And he's staying until he gets the job done.

Are you brave enough to tackle this drawing of ruthless Raditz?

- You know the drill. Start on that stick figure!

- Back to basics! Lay in those shapes. Draw circles where his knees will be and a big sweeping curve for the hair.

- You're on detail duty! Take your time and don't forget to draw in the Scouter on Raditz's eye. Running into some trouble? You might want to step back and practice drawing the way the head connects to the neck.

- Erase the guidelines and any other lines you don't need. Make sure you've got all the details down. Then do a check of the proportions.

ANDROIDS 17 & 18

* *

Androids were created to be the ultimate fighting machines. These two super-strong teenage androids are the toughest of the bunch. They've come back from the future on a seek-and-destroy mission to take Goku down.

This girl-boy duo will take great pleasure in destroying the Earth unless Trunks, Goku, and the gang can stop them!

- The trick to drawing two characters together is to think about how they look in relation to one another. For example, the top of Android 17's head comes up to Android 18's eye line. Android 17's feet are a little bigger than 18's feet. The center lines for both figures are parallel.

- This step doesn't change just because there are two figures. Lightly sketch the basic shapes. Notice how they tilt toward each other. Remember, the first two steps are about being fast and loose. Use quick, light lines!

- This drawing has double the details. Get to it! Don't forget the logo on Android 18's shirt.

- Did you miss any details? Are both characters about the same size? Then, great job! Clean up your drawing and you're done.

Cell is a vile creature that's one hundred times more lethal and cunning than even the deadly Androids 17 & 18. Not a shock — he was created from the cells of all the best martial arts masters.

Cell is ready to pounce! Set up the stance by sketching the legs wide apart. Then draw a circle for the hips instead of a line. See how his entire face will fall below the shoulder line?

The keys to Cell's creepiness are his spreading wings and winding tail. Add them to your sketch now. Then place the amulet on his forehead right on that center line. In this stage, most of the fingers look like rectangles.

There are lots of details on this vicious villain — especially on his face and buglike torso. Have fun with them!

Clean up your drawing. How did you do? Did you notice the line running through the tail and the extra outline on the wings?

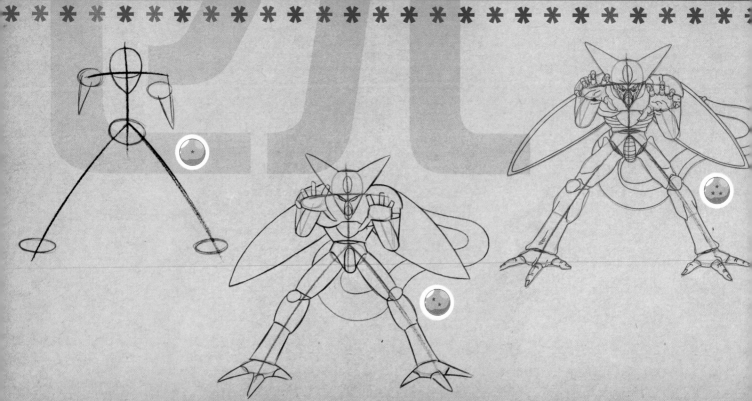

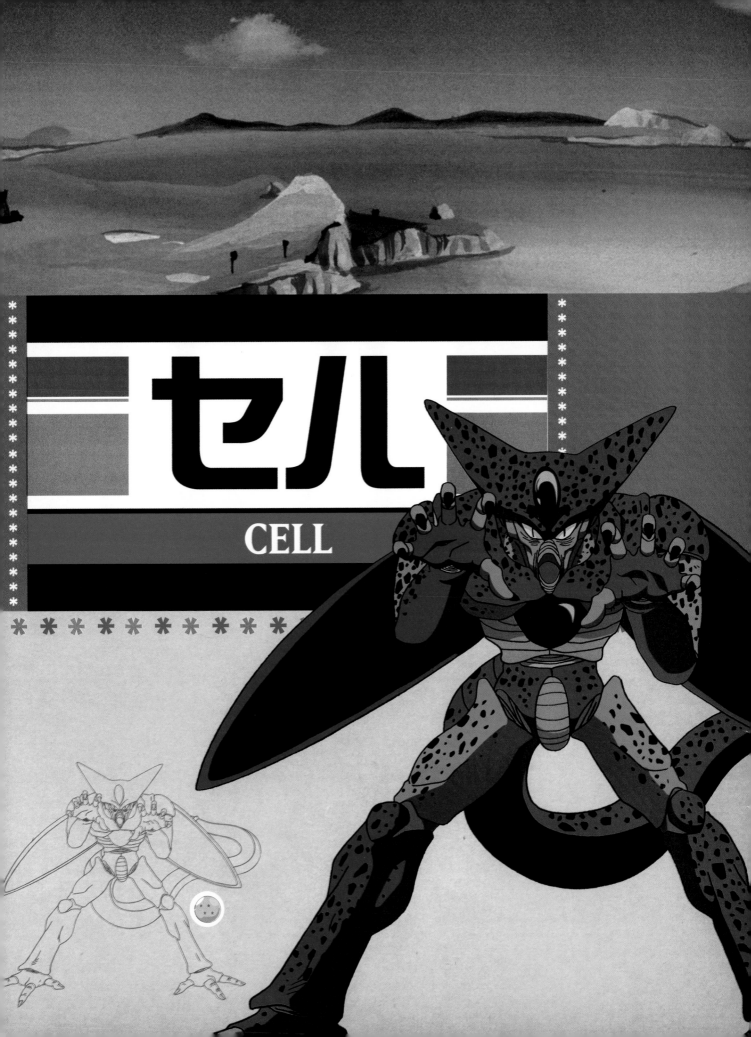

セル

CELL

スーパーサイヤ人
ベジータ

SUPER SAIYAN MAJIN VEGETA

What's up with the M on Vegeta's forehead? That symbol marks him as being under the evil influence of the wizard Babidi. And it's not just a fashion statement. In this state, Vegeta is so strong he could even win a fight against Goku!

Start with a stick figure. The stance is wide — just as in the drawing of Piccolo — and the vertical guideline runs right down the center of Vegeta's body. This time, add circles for the shoulders.

Lightly draw the shapes of the body around the guidelines. Start to draw his snarling face and clenched fists.

Give the outline shape and form. Then add details like the bulging veins all over Vegeta's skin. Don't forget the M on his forehead.

Step back and take a good look at your drawing. Did you add the detail lines in the hair? Do the fists have little lines at the knuckles? Now get out your eraser and clean up this drawing!

Good? Bad? This childlike form of Buu doesn't really know the difference. Or care. He was conjured into existence long ago by the evil wizard Babidi to help destroy the Earth. He can transform from Buu, to Evil Buu, to his incredibly powerful form, SUPER BUU!

 You know what to do! Draw the circle for Majin Buu's head bigger than you did for the other characters. The guideline at his hips is wider than usual to support Buu's bulging belly.

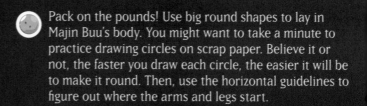 Pack on the pounds! Use big round shapes to lay in Majin Buu's body. You might want to take a minute to practice drawing circles on scrap paper. Believe it or not, the faster you draw each circle, the easier it will be to make it round. Then, use the horizontal guidelines to figure out where the arms and legs start.

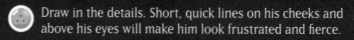 Draw in the details. Short, quick lines on his cheeks and above his eyes will make him look frustrated and fierce.

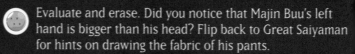 Evaluate and erase. Did you notice that Majin Buu's left hand is bigger than his head? Flip back to Great Saiyaman for hints on drawing the fabric of his pants.

スーパーサイヤ人3
悟空 vs ブウ

SUPER SAIYAN 3 GOKU vs KID BUU

* *

Kid Buu is a pint-size powerhouse who moves from one world to another, destroying everything in his wake. But not if Goku has anything to say about it!

Every drawing challenge so far has been leading up to this final battle. You've worked hard for this. Show off your Super Saiyan skills!

Start with two fighting stick figures. Curve the center line for Kid Buu. This will help you draw the arch in his back. Then make sure you draw the center line for Goku's body much longer than the one for Kid Buu. Goku is bigger than his enemy.

Pay attention to overlapping when you sketch the shapes of the bodies. Kid Buu's left leg falls in front of Goku's right leg. Having trouble? Take a look at the next step. It might give you a better idea of how these shapes come together into a finished drawing.

Don't stress! It may look like there are too many details, but you can handle it. Sketch in Kid Buu's long, curved tentacle. See how Goku is grabbing it in his fist?

Erase any lines you don't need. Then take a good look at your drawing. Compare it to the finished one. Is anything missing on your version? Does anything need a quick fix?

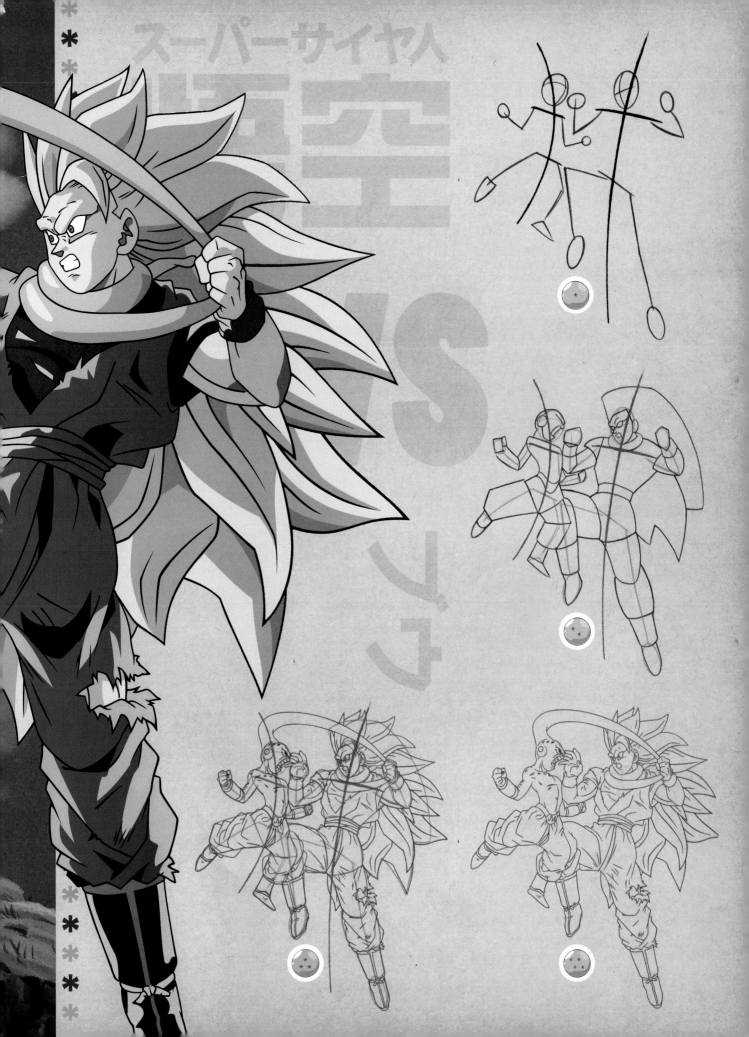

スーパーサイヤ人
孫悟空

CONGRATULATIONS!
You are an official Super Saiyan 3 Drawing Master!

Now that you can draw so many Dragonball Z heroes and villains, it's time to create your own awesome action scenes and power-packed sagas. The safety of the universe is in your hands!